The Common Core Readiness Guide to Reading™

TIPS & TRICKS FOR
ANALYZING
TEXT AND CITING
EVIDENCE

Sandra K. Athans and Robin W. Parente

ROSEN
PUBLISHING®

New York

Published in 2015 by The Rosen Publishing Group, Inc.
29 East 21st Street, New York, NY 10010

Library of Congress Cataloging-in-Publication Data

Athans, Sandra K., 1958– author
Tips & tricks for analyzing text and citing evidence/Sandra K. Athans and Robin W. Parente.—First Edition.pages cm.—(The Common Core Readiness Guide to Reading.)
Includes bibliographical references and index.
Audience: Ages 5-8.
Includes bibliographical references and index.
ISBN 978-1-4777-7539-4 (library bound)—ISBN 978-1-4777-7541-7 (pbk.)—ISBN 978-1-4777-7542-4 (6-pack)
1. Bibliographical citations—Juvenile literature. 2. Authorship—Bibliography. I. Parente, Robin W. II. Title. III. Title: Tips and tricks for analyzing text and citing evidence.
PN171.F56A84 2015
372.47'2—dc23

2013048407

Manufactured in the United States of America

Contents

Introduction

The Common Core Reading Standards are a set of skills designed to prepare you for entering college or beginning your career. They're grouped into broad College and Career Ready Anchor Standards, and they help you use reasoning and evidence in ways that will serve you well now and in the future.

The skills build from kindergarten to the twelfth grade. Grades six through eight take the spotlight here. You may already have noticed changes in your classrooms that are based on the standards—deeper-level reading, shorter passages, an emphasis on informational texts, or an overall increase in rigor within your daily activities.

This book will help you understand, practice, and independently apply the skills through easy-to-use tips and tricks. Gaining mastery of the skills is the goal.

Your teachers may use close reading for some of their instruction. During close reading you read shorter passages more deeply and analytically.

The Anchor Standards help ensure exposure to a range of texts and tasks. They also shape skills necessary for reading increasingly complex texts.

Close reading passages often have rich, complex content. They contain grade-level vocabulary words, sentence structures, and literary techniques. Reading a short, three-page passage closely could take two to three days or more. The benefit to you is that you get a deeper, more valuable understanding of what you've read. Close reading is a critical part of the new Common Core Reading Standards and is used throughout this book.

Other well-known reading comprehension skills remain valuable. Visualizing, asking questions, synthesizing, and other traditional strategies work well together with the Common Core skills covered here.

This book focuses on Anchor Standard 1, Analyzing Text and Citing Evidence. In the next section, we'll break these skills apart and look at them closely. Tips and tricks for using the skills are also explained.

In the passages that follow, you tag along with "expert readers" as they think aloud while close reading from different passages of literature (fiction) and informational text (nonfiction). Ways in which the expert reader applies them appear in expert reader margin notes. You'll also review multiple-choice and written response questions completed by the expert reader.

After you gain an understanding of how the skill is applied, it's your turn to try with guided practice. You'll apply the skill independently and perform a self-evaluation by checking your responses against answers provided. Based on your responses, you can determine if another pass through the expert reader's examples might be helpful—or if you've mastered the skill.

CHAPTER 1

A QUICK AND EASY OVERVIEW: THE SKILLS AND THE TIPS AND TRICKS

Let's examine the skills involved with analyzing text and citing evidence closely so that we understand them. We know that the word "analyze" is a verb, so it's something we actively do. When you analyze while reading, you carefully examine, inspect, and consider the text in order to fully understand it. As you analyze text you must rely on its content—not on knowledge you gained elsewhere. Sometimes you may have to break text down into smaller, more manageable units, such as sentences or paragraphs, in order to understand it more fully.

You may also need to make inferences about ideas or events not explicitly stated. An inference is a conclusion you make by interpreting clues provided in the passage—it's as if you're reading between the lines. Your inferences must be reasonably based on something concrete in the text.

Evidence is information from the text that a reader uses to prove something, like a position on a topic, a conclusion or inference, the main idea of a text, and more. Citing evidence for your ideas—whether you're sharing them through writing or speaking—is a critical component of this standard.

Reading texts closely and analytically builds engagement and a deeper level of understanding of literature and informational texts.

These skills are useful as you read literature and informational text and in reading within history/social studies, science, and technical subjects. They're also useful for many of your daily real-life activities.

As you progress in grade levels, you're expected to use multiple pieces of evidence to support your analysis, identify the strongest evidence that supports your analysis, and apply the skill to primary and secondary source materials.

Analysis Tips and Tricks

There are several easy-to-use tips and tricks that can help you analyze reading passages. Some are useful as you begin to read, while others guide you throughout your reading. Here's a quick overview of them. In the next sections, you'll see how they're used in action with literature and informational texts. The icons are used in subsequent chapters to cue you into the use of the tips and tricks.

● **Launching "Jump-Start" Clues** – Before you dive into reading a piece of text, skim and scan it quickly. Notice and take a visual inventory of everything you see. The title, subheadings, boldface print, and other features like photographs or charts will give you valuable clues about the content and genre. Authors select and use text features purposefully. It's often helpful to ask yourself: *What could the title mean or what purpose do the special features serve?*

● **Using Genre and Text Structure (Flexibly) to Build and Check Understanding** – You already know a lot about the different genres and their structures. For example, in works of fiction, characters and a setting are introduced, a problem is identified, and events lead to a solution or improvement. With informational text, authors organize ideas into cause and effect or other structures that help readers grasp and remember important information. Working with these structures to guide and validate your understanding and analysis is helpful. You might ask yourself: *Does the story unfold in a way that makes sense, or does the information seem valid and cohesive?*

Quick Check Self-Evaluation for Analyzing Texts

Determining how well you've mastered the tips and tricks for analyzing text is important. One way to do this is by gauging your success with the following tasks:

✓ I can summarize the passage.

✓ My summary is cohesive and makes sense based on evidence.

✓ I can identify important details and the author's message.

✓ My ideas can be supported using specific examples from the text.

✓ Look for the icons in subsequent chapters to see how this checklist is used in action.

● **Identifying a Point of View or Perspective** – Thinking about who is telling the story or who is presenting information also gives you insight. In fiction, a story often unfolds through the eyes of a character (first person) or narrator (third person). Nonfiction and informational text is filtered through someone's perspective. Knowing this may be important as you analyze text, especially as you consider the credibility of a fictional character or a "knowledgeable" source. It's helpful to think about what insights you, the reader, have. It may be necessary for you to use evidence-based inferencing—or reading between the lines—to explain actions, events, or ideas that are not explicitly stated.

● **Tune in to Your Inside Voice** – Your mind is actively making sense as you read. Listening to your thoughts or your mind's dialogue helps

Quick Check Self-Evaluation for Locating and Citing Evidence

Determining how well you've mastered the tips and tricks for citing evidence is important. One way to do this is by gauging your success with the following tasks:

√ I can support my views with text-based examples.

√ I've identified my strongest evidence and presented it well.

√ I've used multiple pieces of evidence, especially for my inferential thinking.

√ My interpretation aligns with what the author likely intended.

√ Look for the icons in subsequent chapters to see how this checklist is used in action.

you grasp meaning. Connecting new ideas to known ideas is the way your mind builds cohesive meaning. Monitoring your thoughts, including your questions, is critical. Do events, actions, and ideas seem unusual or out of place? Are your reactions likely what the author intended? Authors often build reader engagement by posing questions. However, it's also important for you to distinguish when you're confused and need to implement fix-up strategies like rereading.

● **Avoid Common Pitfalls** – Sometimes we can become distracted by something in the text, which could steer us away from an author's intended meaning. Staying engaged and focused while ensuring that your ideas square with evidence is critical. It's sometimes helpful to validate your interpretation by considering how you would complete the following statement: *I know this because....*

Sharing ideas with others can be a valuable way to strengthen analytical skills. Using discussion to think through an author's intention, the validity of a piece of text evidence, or other analytical matters can be very valuable.

As you practice and gain skill with these tips and tricks, you'll find that they work together and often become indistinguishable. This is a sure sign that they've become authentic and automatic and kick in when and where they're needed.

Locating and Citing Evidence Tips and Tricks

There are also some easy-to-use tips and tricks to help you spot and use evidence effectively. Here's a quick overview of them. In the next sections, you'll see how evidence is used during reading and also as a way to demonstrate understanding of a passage through multiple-choice and short answer questions.

- **Using Key Events and/or Direct Quotations as Evidence** – Identifying why and how you think, feel, or construct ideas from a passage is based on text evidence. Sometimes the evidence is clear through events, explanations, character dialogue, or other ways that are explicit. In informational texts, facts and details are good types of evidence. Extracting this evidence from a passage may be all it takes.

- **Building Evidence for Inferential Thinking** – When information is implied but not explicitly stated, you base your thoughts, feelings, and views on clues. Returning to the passage and locating these clues is how you **build a case** for your ideas. Making sure your ideas align or square with text clues ensures that you're interpreting the passage in a way the author likely intended. This is critical.

- **Sizing-Up the Quantity, Quality, and Order of Your Evidence** – Not all evidence is the same. Knowing how strong one piece of evidence is against another helps you determine which is best to use to support your views. It could also suggest an order for how you present your evidence. Returning to the text to carefully consider these matters is helpful.

• **Avoid Common Pitfalls** – Misinterpreting any part of the text can occur when your thinking doesn't square with text evidence. Always ask yourself if your thinking is most likely what the author intended.

CHAPTER 2

ANALYZING TEXT AND CITING EVIDENCE IN LITERATURE: EXPERT READER MODEL

Let's see how to apply the tips and tricks to literature. Remember literature could be adventure stories, historical fiction, mysteries, myths, science fiction, realistic fiction, allegories, parodies, satire, drama, graphic novels, one-act and multi-act plays, narrative poems, lyrical poems, free-verse poems, sonnets, odes, ballads and epics, and more.

Literature often features elements such as characters, problems or conflicts, a setting and plot, events and episodes, and a problem resolution. Awareness of the structure helps a reader follow the story and improves comprehension of the passage.

Specific genres within literature also have specific characteristics and features. For example, science fiction contains elements of the supernatural, and dramatic plays contain scripted character dialogue. Your ability to analyze literature and use evidence relies on your grade-level knowledge of literature basics.

Works of literature include a variety of genres, each with unique characteristics. Determining the genre of a passage can jump-start the analysis process.

Plan of Action

The passage in this chapter is an excerpt from *The Odyssey: An Adventure Classic*. You'll be reading the passage and following as an expert reader thinks through a sampling of the tips and tricks in margin notes. It's as if you're tagging along with the expert reader.

You'll also observe the expert reader perform a self-evaluation by sharing a summary and the thinking behind it. You'll also tag along through some multiple-choice and constructed response questions to get the full impact of the expert reader's use of text evidence.

Then, it's your turn to practice. You'll be reading a second passage where guided practice prompts cue your use of the tips and tricks. You can check your thinking against the provided responses.

🏃 An Excerpt from *The Odyssey: An Adventure Classic*
Retold by Pauline Francis

Introduction

The Odyssey is a 12,000-line poem written by a Greek poet called Homer at end of the eighth century BC. It tells the story of the return of Odysseus—King of Ithaca—from the Trojan War. When the Greeks had defeated and burned Troy, the Greek leaders led their own ships home. Odysseus took many years to reach his home in Ithaca—years full of suffering and great danger. 🪜

🔖 EXPERT READER:

🏃 From scanning the passage, I think this could be a classic Greek myth. The introduction will give me more insights. From clues (on next page), I can see this is the first chapter in a multi-chapter book. I know a Cyclops is a one-eyed monster.

🪜 The introduction confirms my thinking about genre. *The Odyssey* is a Greek epic poem. I can expect realistic and imaginary events involving the Greek gods will likely occur. Odysseus is probably the main character. He'll probably encounter a dangerous Cyclops.

Chapter 1: The Cyclops

When Odysseus and his twelve ships sailed home from the Trojan War, they faced many dangers on the islands where they stopped to find food and water. And at sea, they faced terrible storms.

On the tenth day of their journey, they came to land again. Opposite the harbor was a wooded island, inhabited by wild goats.

"We shall stay here," Odysseus commanded, "until I find out what dangers may await us on the mainland."

When they had eaten, Odysseus, and twelve of his best men, crossed to the mainland. Here they came to an empty cave, surrounded by a stone wall, which held many lambs. Taking food and wine, they went into the cave and lit a fire.

Toward sunset, they heard the sound of sheep outside. A shadow fell over the entrance to the cave. Odysseus saw a monster, with only one enormous eye in the middle of his forehead, herding his sheep into the cave.

"NO!" Odysseus whispered to his men. "We have come to the land of the Cyclopes. They are the one-eyed sons of Poseidon, the sea god. They are fierce people who live in mountain caves. They have *no* sense of right or wrong."

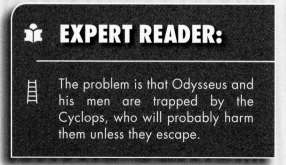

EXPERT READER:

The problem is that Odysseus and his men are trapped by the Cyclops, who will probably harm them unless they escape.

The monster pulled an enormous rock across the entrance to the cave, so that his sheep could not escape. Then he lit a fire and sat down. Suddenly, in the firelight, the Cyclops caught sight of Odysseus and his men.

"Strangers!" he bellowed. "Who are you?"

"We are Greeks," Odysseus replied, "who have been besieging Troy these last nine years. Now we are sailing home, but we have been blown off our course. Good sir, we seek your kindness. Our god is Zeus, and he is the god of guests."

"Stranger, you must be a fool," the Cyclops boomed. "We Cyclopes care *nothing* for the gods—except for our father, Poseidon."

As he spoke, he picked up two of the men and beat their heads on the ground. Then he tore them to pieces and devoured them, like a mountain lion. The others wept as they watched, and prayed to Zeus.

> **🔖 EXPERT READER:**
>
> Wow, although this is graphic, this is typical of this genre.

"There is no point in killing him," Odysseus said to himself, "for we shall not be able to move the rock to escape from this terrible place."

The next morning, the Cyclops ate two more of Odysseus' companions. Then he drove his sheep outside and blocked up the entrance once more. Odysseus, with murder in his heart, had an idea. The Cyclops had left behind his wooden stick, as tall as a ship's mast. 𝒯

"Sharpen the end!" he commanded his men, "And hide it!"

> **🔖 EXPERT READER:**
>
> 𝒯 A narrator tells the story, but I know Odysseus' motives from clues like "with murder in his heart." I'm unsure about other things like how Odysseus' idea is going to unfold.

That evening, when the Cyclops came back with his flock once more, he snatched up two men for his evening meal. Odysseus offered him wine to wash down their flesh.

"What is your name?" the Cyclops asked Odysseus.

"Nobody," Odysseus replied, offering him more wine.

The Cyclops drank until he toppled to the ground, asleep.

At once, Odysseus thrust the enormous stick into the fire and, when it was hot, he hammered it into the Cyclops' eye. It hissed like hot metal does when a smith plunges it into cold water. The Cyclops woke up, uttered a terrible shriek and pulled out the stake. Other

EXPERT READER:

Now the plan makes sense to me!

Cyclopes living nearby came to see what was wrong.

"Polyphemus!" they called. "Why do you spoil our sleep with all this noise?"

"Nobody is killing me!" he cried.

Odysseus sailed for many years to reach his home in Ithaca following the defeat of Troy in the Trojan War. *The Odyssey* tells the story of his journey.

"Then you are a fool," they laughed.

The blind Cyclops, moaning with pain, pushed the rock from the mouth of the cave, and sat across the entrance.

"Now I'll catch them as they leave my cave!" he thought.

Another plan formed in Odysseus' head. He commanded his men to lash the sheep together—three at a time—with willow branches from the giant's bed. Each man tied him-self under the belly of the middle sheep. In this way, they all were able to escape from the cave. They ran to their boat and set sail for the island. The Cyclops was so angry that he hurled a rock at them and almost washed them back to the mainland.

"Cyclops!" Odysseus shouted. "If anyone ever asks how you came to be blind, tell them you were blinded by Odysseus."

Reaching the island again, they sacrificed to Zeus the big ram that had carried Odysseus from the cave. And when dawn appeared, they sailed on.

They left with heavy hearts, grieving for the dear friends they had lost, but glad at their own escape from death.

As they came close to Ithaca, their ships were blown by strong winds to another island full of tall men who hurled rocks down onto them. And

EXPERT READER:

I can confirm Odysseus's role as main character. I also learn about him—he's a clever leader who commands his men bravely and passionately.

The events in the story unfold sequentially around Odysseus' plan.

EXPERT READER:

Odysseus' loyalty to the gods is revealed several times throughout the story. This is in sharp contrast to the Cyclops, who belittles all gods but Poseidon.

The solution is that Odysseus escaped from the dangers of the Cyclops, but he lost many men and is remorseful.

EXPERT READER:

⚠ I'm going to reread earlier parts of the passage because I don't recall the Cyclops praying. Either I missed it or Odysseus infers this was done.

out of the twelve ships, only one was left.

"Poseidon has answered the prayer of his son, the Cyclops," Odysseus wept. ⚠

Quick Check Self-Evaluation for Analyzing Texts

Let's take a break here to let the expert reader summarize and analyze this passage.

Based on my analysis of this text, I know it describes Odysseus' adventures of escape from the Cyclops. Through cleverness, trickery, bravery, and his devotion to Zeus, Odysseus is able to defeat the Cyclops and return on his quest homeward. Odysseus' victory over the Cyclops is also filled with sadness. He loses many ships and men during his escape, and he angers Poseidon, who seeks revenge. The main idea is that bravery, intelligence, and devotion are valuable, especially when tackling very difficult challenges. They also can bring comfort in times of sadness.

Expert Reader: I'm satisfied with this summary. I thought about the passage carefully, I reread some sections to check my understanding against text evidence, and I used key ideas to support my ideas. I'm ready to challenge my thinking by answering multiple-choice and constructed response questions.

Rely on text evidence when completing multiple-choice or constructed response questions. Returning to the passage several times may be necessary.

Quick Check Self-Evaluation for Locating and Citing Evidence

Notice that in some cases more than one answer could be considered correct. It is important to use evidence to build a case for the *best* answer. Carefully reviewing evidence by returning to the passage will be helpful. Then gauging which response is best supported through the evidence is critical.

Mini Assessment

1. Odysseus deceives Polyphemus and claims his name is Nobody. What problem did Odysseus foresee and overcome by doing this? Base your answer on evidence.

a) Odysseus suspects Polyphemus might summon other Cyclopes for help.

b) Odysseus feared Polyphemus might side with the people of Troy and kill him.

c) Odysseus thought Polyphemus' knowledge of his identify could trigger conflict between Poseidon and Zeus.

d) Odysseus knew the Cyclopes would be jealous of his relationship with Zeus and kill him.

2. How is Odysseus' escape plan best described?

a) It reflects Odysseus' skill at devising solutions from start to finish.

b) It demonstrates Odysseus' knowledge of available resources on remote islands.

c) It shows how Odysseus often relied on Zeus for help.

d) It reflects Odysseus' quick-thinking ability to shape a step-by-step plan.

3. Which statement is not supported in the story?

a) Despite Odysseus' struggles, his commitment to Zeus was unwavering.

Odysseus faced endless challenges and danger on his homeward journey. Many of his struggles are depicted in Greek artwork.

b) Polyphemus is amused by Odysseus' plea for kindness.

c) Odysseus is caught off guard by Polyphemus' acts of brutality.

d) Polyphemus sought his father's revenge against Odysseus.

Check your answers. Were you correct?

1. a) is the best answer. Polyphemus cries out "Nobody is killing me!" after Odysseus blinds him. Polyphemus hopes other Cyclopes will aid him. Yet his plea makes no sense, and the Cyclopes laugh. Although Odysseus' motive is not explicit, text-based clues support this answer.

2. d) is the best answer. Odysseus' plan is crafted in stages. Once he is successful at blinding and tricking the Cyclops, he devises a way to escape beneath the sheep. The sentence "Another plan formed in Odysseus' head" supports that the plan was composed in parts.

3. b) is the best answer. The narrator expresses that Polyphemus "booms" his response to Odysseus, calls him a fool, and devours two of Odysseus' men. These responses do not suggest amusement. Responses a, c, and d can be supported with text evidence.

Expert Reader: I'm satisfied with my responses. In all cases, I returned to the text to check against evidence. Sometimes, the evidence was right there—explicit in a character's actions or words. Other times, I had to dig a little deeper and use clues and inferences. In either case, my answers square with the evidence. Now I feel I'm ready to try a constructed response question.

Question: How does Odysseus embody ideal characteristic of greatness? What could this suggest about life and times in ancient Greece? Use evidence from the passage to support your answer.

Odysseus is a brave and intelligent leader. He is a master at developing plans that are clever, daring, and resourceful. For example, he conquers a fierce opponent, the Cyclops, by blinding and tricking him. Then, he and his men cleverly escape beneath the belly of the sheep. Odysseus is also compassionate. He weeps openly when his men are harmed, and he prepares to avenge their death with murder (even though this does not happen). Likewise, many of his actions demonstrate his devotion to Zeus. Specifically, he names Zeus as his god, he prays to Zeus, and he sacrificed a ram to honor him. Odysseus' traits, as well as his compassion and devotion, would be considered virtues and ideal characteristics of greatness. These would have helped guide the people of Greece in the 8th Century BCE through battles and other challenges such as loss and tragedy. Based on the genre and format, Homer likely intended that these ideals be shared aloud with others to unite and guide the people of Greece. 📖

Conclusion

How well have you grasped the expert reader's use of the tips and tricks to analyze text and cite evidence in literature? Decide if you're ready to move on to the guided practice in the next chapter or if you would like to take another pass through the expert reader's model.

📖 EXPERT READER:

📖 Odysseus characterized greatness through his bravery, intelligence, compassion, and devotion. I use specific examples that support my claims and ordered them based on their importance to the plot of the story. Also, I know that epics were used to teach people basic lessons. This idea squared with my analysis of the story. My understanding is likely what the author intended.

CHAPTER 3

ANALYZING TEXT AND CITING EVIDENCE IN LITERATURE: GUIDED PRACTICE

Now it's time for you to apply the tips and tricks during your close reading of a passage. The practice prompt icons will guide you. Check to see if your responses to the prompts match possible responses provided.

As a story unfolds, it may be necessary to rethink, reshape, or completely change a view or idea. Maintaing an open mind and a willingness to revise ideas is critical.

🏃 An Excerpt from *The Odyssey: An Adventure Classic*

Chapter 2: A Wicked Enchantress

GUIDED PRACTICE PROMPT:

🏃 What jump-start clues do you notice? (Possible response: From the headings, I notice this passage continues *The Odyssey*. Instead of a Cyclops, Odysseus will battle an evil enchantress. Although I'm uncertain what or who this enchantress is, I'm certain I'll find out.)

Odysseus and his surviving men came to another island. Silently, they brought their ship into harbor. Then, exhausted, they rested on the beach for two days. At dawn, on the third day, Odysseus took his spear and sword and left the ship. He climbed to the top of a hill, from where he saw smoke amongst the trees.

"I do not know what dangers are here," he thought. "I shall return to the ship to feast. Then I shall explore the island with my men."

On his way back to the shore, Odysseus killed a stag and they feasted the whole of the day and night. At dawn, Odysseus divided his men into two groups: one led by him, the other by Eurylochus. After drawing lots, it was Eurylochus who set off first, taking twenty-two men with him.

GUIDED PRACTICE PROMPT:

What do you notice about the genre and its structure? (Possible response: I can confirm this passage continues *The Odyssey*. There is also a pattern—Odysseus and his men land on an island where unknown danger awaits, they rest, and then set off to explore.)

Eurylochus did not return until dusk—and he was alone. He could hardly utter a word. At last, he spoke. "We came to a beautiful house built of stone," he wept. "There were lions and wolves prowling around it, but they did not harm us. A woman was sitting in the porch, singing as she wove her tapestry.

GUIDED PRACTICE PROMPT:

What are you thinking? (Possible response: This woman could be the wicked enchantress, but I'll have to read on to confirm this.)

How is the text structure helping you here? (Possible response: The problem in this story is that Eurylochus' men were turned into pigs and held in a pigsty.)

GUIDED PRACTICE PROMPT:

What are you thinking? (Possible response: I wonder why Hermes is helping? Maybe because he is messenger of the gods, I can infer that the gods are watching out for Odysseus. I can also confirm that Circe, the woman Eurylochus encountered earlier, is indeed the enchantress.)

When she caught sight of us, she invited us to eat and drink with her. But I did not trust her. So I stood guard outside."

"What happened?" Odysseus asked, his heart sinking. "Where are the others?"

"The...the woman gave them cups of wine...then she touched them with a wooden stick." Eurylochus shuddered. "They sprouted bristles and dropped to the ground. She changed them into pigs! Then she laughed and drove them into a pigsty."

Odysseus picked up his bow and sword. "Come," he said. "We must go to that house and free them."

"I cannot go with you!" Eurylochus wept.

"Then stay here and rest," Odysseus replied. "I shall go alone." As he made his way through the forest, Odysseus met Hermes, the messenger of the gods.

"Have you come to free your men from the enchantress, Circe?" he asked Odysseus. "You must let me help, or you, too, will meet the same fate as them." He stopped to pick a plant growing close by—a wild garlic. "If you drink this, it will protect you from Circe's evil. When she has given you her magic potion, she will tap you with her stick.

But her potion will have no power over you. At that same moment, you must draw your sword, as if you mean to kill her. She will beg forgiveness and you can ask her to undo the wrong she has done to your men."

Odysseus did as Hermes instructed. And when he took his sword to threaten the enchantress, she was amazed. "No man has ever resisted my magic powers," she cried. "Are you Odysseus? Hermes told me once that you would come this way from Troy!"

Circe commanded food and drink to be brought, and servants to wash Odysseus. But he shook his head. "How can I accept what you offer when my men are still in your pigsty?" he asked.

Circe went at once to the pigsty and drove out the pigs. Then she smeared ointment on their backs. At once, they became men again, and they greeted Odysseus with tears of joy. And Circe persuaded Odysseus to fetch his companions from the ship to rest and feast. Everybody came, except for Eurylochus. Odysseus would have slain him in anger, if the others had not prevented him. So he stayed behind to guard the ship.

The days passed in feasting and resting and they did not realize that a whole year had passed by. At last, Odysseus' companions persuaded him that it was time to sail on to Ithaca. He went to break the news to Circe.

GUIDED PRACTICE PROMPT:

What are you thinking? (Possible response: Odysseus' loyalty to his men is also evident in this myth.)

GUIDED PRACTICE PROMPT:

What are you thinking? (Possible response: Odysseus seems distracted from his quest to return to Ithaca. I think the enchantress's magic powers caused this. There's evidence to support this, such as Odysseus needs persuading to leave and has to break the news to Circe, so he must be concerned about her feelings.)

GUIDED PRACTICE PROMPT:

How is the text structure helping you here? (Possible response: As this is a second passage about Odysseus, I'm building my understanding of *The Odyssey*. The stories are similar in many ways. Odysseus' route home is unclear, he lands on islands, faces challenges, and sails on.)

"Leave, if that is what you wish," Circe said. "But I do not know the way to Ithaca. To find out how to get there, you must consult the prophet Tiresias. Only he has the knowledge that you need."

"Where shall I find him?" Odysseus asked.

"In the Underworld," Circe replied. "In the Land of the Dead."

Odysseus' heart almost broke at her words. "Nobody has ever sailed a black ship into the Underworld and come back," he said.

"Listen!" Circe replied. "I shall tell you what to do when you get there."

The men, thinking they were going home, prepared to sail—all except a young man called Elpenor, who was sleeping on the roof. As he hurried to join the others, he missed his footing and fell, breaking his neck.

When Odysseus told his men that they were going to the Underworld, they were heartbroken. But they sailed on, leaving their ship at the dark place where the two rivers of the dead flowed into one another.

Quick Check Self-Evaluation for Analyzing Texts

At this point, you should be able to summarize the story and think about the meaning the author intended. What is the strongest evidence that may lead you to the author's message? Go ahead and try it! Talk it through or get a piece of paper and write it down and then check out the expert reader's take.

Once you're satisfied and have checked your responses, challenge your thinking and answer the multiple-choice and constructed response questions that follow.

Expert Reader's Summary: This passage describes Odysseus' adventures of escape from Circe, an evil enchantress. With help from Hermes, Odysseus avoids falling under Circe's evil spell and is able to save his men, whom Circe turned into pigs and held captive in a pigsty. However, Odysseus loses track of time and stays on the island with Circe and his men for over a year. He was distracted from his intent to return to Ithaca. In my first analysis, I think the evidence suggests that Odysseus was affected by Circe's magic, which was a different kind of danger than in the Cyclops story. Still, Odysseus was victorious and escaped to begin another adventure on his journey home to Ithaca.

Quick Check Self-Evaluation for Citing Evidence: Mini Assessment

Read and respond to each question. Then, check your answers in the section that follows.

1. What evidence supports the statement that Odysseus valued strong leadership?

a) Odysseus listened to Hermes as he was sent from the gods to guide Odysseus safely off Circe's island.

b) Odysseus was unwilling to forgive Eurylochus for endangering his men.

c) Odysseus thought his men were weak for following Eurylochus.

d) Nothing happened to the men that Odysseus led on Circe's island, so he was clearly the stronger leader.

2. In the last paragraph, Elpenor is introduced into the story. Evidence suggesting that his role may be to foreshadow events that could happen in another adventure include all of the following except...

a) Elpenor's role is unclear.

b) Odysseus' reaction to Elpenor's death seems out of character.

c) Elpenor's death and Odysseus' need to travel to the Land of the Dead is an unusual coincidence.

d) Odysseus found Elpenor lazy.

3. Reread the last paragraph. Describe the tone of the paragraph and identify the details that contribute to this.

a) The tone is carefree because the men were relieved to survive Circe's evil spell.

b) The tone is somber because no one ever returned from the Underworld.

c) The tone is somber as the men are heartbroken, the setting is dark, and they must leave their ship behind.

d) The tone is uplifting as the men agreed to travel on even though they don't want to.

Check your answers. Were you correct?

1. b) can be supported by the evidence. Odysseus' anger grew over Eurylochus' inability to take leadership of the men, both on the island and also during their rescue. He had to be prevented from killing him.

2. d) is the correct answer as it is the exception and doesn't support Elpenor's role in foreshadowing future events.

3. c) is the correct answer as the claim and evidence appear in the last paragraph and are well matched. There is no evidence supporting a and b in the last paragraph. In response to d, the claim and evidence are not well aligned.

What do you think so far? Is your understanding and analysis of the passage taking shape? Did you return to the passage and find evidence to support your responses? Did your answers square with the evidence? Are you comfortable discussing or writing a response to the following constructed response question?

Question: In this story, Odysseus faces different kinds of dangers. Using evidence from the passage, identify these dangers and describe how they are different from one another. How do these dangers contribute to the main idea of the passage?

As you prepare your response, keep in mind the following:
- Have you supported your views with text-based examples?
- Is your strongest evidence presented first?
- Have you provided multiple pieces of evidence, especially if you're using inferential thinking?
- Does your interpretation align with what the author likely intended?

Once you're satisfied with your response, see how the expert reader responded. You may have a different view. That's OK as long as it holds up under scrutiny and squares with the text evidence you've chosen.

Possible Response: Odysseus faces many dangers in this passage. The first is that Circe captures Odysseus' men, turns them into pigs, and holds them captive in a pigsty. She also intends to do the same to

Odysseus. The first danger Odysseus must overcome is freeing his men, while not falling victim to Circe's magic spell. The second danger is losing sight of his mission to return home. He is distracted by feasting and resting and is unaware that a year passes. These dangers are very different. In the first, Odysseus' life is endangered. In the second, Odysseus' sense of purpose is threatened. Hermes helps Odysseus resolve the first, and Odysseus' men help him resolve the second. The main idea that danger can take many forms is demonstrated in the story. Additionally, methods of resolving danger may also vary.

Conclusion

How well have you grasped the tips and tricks to analyze text and cite evidence in literature? Based on your performance and self-evaluation, decide if you're ready to move on to the next section or if you would like to take another pass through this guided practice.

CHAPTER 4

ANALYZING TEXT AND CITING EVIDENCE IN INFORMATIONAL TEXT: EXPERT READER MODEL

Now, let's see how to apply the tips and tricks to informational text. Remember informational text is a type of nonfiction, or factual, text, which is written to inform or to give facts about the arts, sciences, or social studies. Informational text can include newspaper and magazine articles, essays, graphs and charts, opinion pieces, memoirs, and historical, scientific, technical, or economic accounts.

Authors of informational text frequently organize their ideas by using a problem/solution, descriptive, compare/contrast, chronological/sequential or cause/effect text structure. Awareness of the structure helps a reader remember information and improves comprehension of text.

Plan of Action

The passage in this chapter is an excerpt from *Atlantis and Other Lost Worlds*. You'll be reading the passage while following as an expert reader thinks through the tips and tricks—this time as they are applied to informational texts.

Again, you'll observe the expert reader perform a self-evaluation through the sharing of a summary and the thinking behind it. Finally, you'll tag along while the expert reader works through some multiple-choice and constructed response questions to get the full impact of the use of text evidence.

Then, it will be your turn to practice. You'll start by reading a passage where guided practice prompts and icons cue your use of the tips and tricks. You can check your thinking against the responses provided.

🏃 An Excerpt from *Atlantis and Other Lost Worlds*
by John Hawkins

🏃 EXPERT READER:

The use of text features and the fact that the text begins with a question suggests this is informational text. Bolded text must be important. Subheadings will help me summarize.

What Was Atlantis?
According to legend, Atlantis was a beautiful, rich, and powerful island nation. It was described by the ancient Greek philosopher Plato in about 360 BC as lying "beyond the Pillars of Hercules" (the Straits of Gibraltar). However, according to Plato, in the middle of a war between Atlantis and Mediterranean countries in 9000 BC, the island sank into the sea in a single day and night.

Imperial City
According to Plato, the island of Atlantis was mountainous and lushly forested. South of Mount Atlas, its towering dormant volcano, was a

fertile plain irrigated by a network of canals. South of the plain was the city of Atlantis, capital of a mighty oceanic empire. The city of Atlantis, Plato records, was composed of circles of land and water connected by bridged canals. Each artificial island was surrounded by high walls and mighty watchtowers. The smallest central island contained the imperial palace and magnificent temple of the sea god, Poseidon, legendary founder of Atlantis.

> **EXPERT READER:**
>
> The author has supplied background and descriptive information in the first few paragraphs. He's also used words like "legend" and phrases such as "According to Plato" to signal that concrete information about Atlantis may be lacking. I've confirmed this is informational text.

Following the collapse of ancient Greek and Roman civilization, Plato's story of Atlantis was dismissed and forgotten. However, this story of a lost island was revived in the 17th century by the German Jesuit priest Athanasius Kircher.

Kircher's Map

Athanasius Kircher was the first scholar to seriously study the Atlantis legend. His research led him to the immense collection of ancient sources at the Vatican Library. Here he came across a well-preserved leather map of Atlantis.  The map had come to Rome from Egypt in the first century AD, but Kircher believed it had been made in the fourth century BC, during Plato's time. The map shows Atlantis as a large island.

> **EXPERT READER:**
>
> The author's choice of words ("scholar," "seriously study," "research," "Vatican Library") lends authority to the discussion and makes me think deeper: Could Atlantis have existed?

It shows a high, centrally located volcano, most likely representing Mount Atlas, along with six major rivers.

Examining the Evidence

EXPERT READER:

The author is using a question/answer type of format that allows me to ponder ideas and then examine evidence. He is using a descriptive structure.

EXPERT READER:

The author has provided me with several possibilities to mull over. I will need to sift through the information to reach a conclusion about the existence of Atlantis.

Did Atlantis Exist?

The legend of Atlantis has been a source of fascination ever since it was rediscovered by the scholars in the 17th century. But did the island ever actually exist? Atlantologists (seekers of Atlantis) argue that a large landmass may once have existed in the location of the Mid-Atlantic Ridge. The Ridge certainly suffers from earthquakes and volcanoes. However, most Plato scholars believe that this Atlantis was imaginary. Plato's story could have been inspired by the fate of the island of Santorini in the Mediterranean. Santorini was destroyed by a volcanic eruption in about 1600 BC.

The Search for Atlantis: The Northeast Atlantic

In 1949, Dr. Maurice Ewing, aboard the research vessel *Glomar Challenger*, found an ocean-floor formation in the Northeast Atlantic, later dubbed the Horseshoe Seamounts. It was made up of a large mound ringed by a range of mountains. Its highest peak was a volcano that had collapsed beneath the sea in the past 12,000 years. Could

If Atlantis really did exist, no one knows what destroyed it. Some experts speculate it might have been an asteroid.

this have been the large island surrounded by a ring of mountains described by Plato?

Expeditions to the undersea mound have retrieved freshwater sand, algae, and rocks that had been formed on dry land, all

📖 EXPERT READER:

Does this discovery provide evidence that may make sense? It seems to be located in the area Plato referenced when describing Atlantis (Straits of Gibraltar).

EXPERT READER:

The author has used evidence in these last two paragraphs to support the existence of Atlantis, but I'm not totally convinced yet.

of which suggested that it had once been an island. Even elephant bones have been dredged from the area, seeming to tie in with Plato's story that these creatures had inhabited Atlantis. In 1974, cameras captured a series of images resembling the partial remains of human-made ruins. Most appeared around the peak of Mount Ampere.

Quick Check Self-Evaluation for Analyzing Texts

Let's take a break here to let the expert reader summarize and analyze this passage so far.

Based on my first analysis of this text, I know that for many centuries, people have been exploring the possibility of the existence of an island nation known as Atlantis. The Greek philosopher Plato told of how Atlantis sank into the sea in a single day and night and while Atlantologists believe this, many scholars who study Plato believe his story was imaginary. An underwater formation has been discovered on the bottom of the Northeast Atlantic Ocean that may or may not match the description Plato gave of Atlantis. The main idea of this text so far is that no one has been able to prove that Atlantis did, in fact, exist.

EXPERT READER:

I think I'm on track with the author. I've thought about the passage carefully, and I've reread sections to check my understanding against text evidence. I'm satisfied my summary is cohesive, includes key details, and makes sense.

According to Plato, Atlantis was composed of artificial islands connected by bridged canals. On the central island was the imperial palace and the temple of the sea god, Poseidon.

Expert Reader: I'm satisfied with this summary. I thought about the passage carefully, I reread some sections to check my understanding against text evidence, and I used key ideas to support my ideas. I'm ready to challenge my thinking by answering multiple-choice and constructed response questions.

Mini Assessment

1. Why did the author most probably include the information in the introductory paragraph?

a) This paragraph was included to explain who Plato was.

b) This paragraph was included to describe how Atlantis disappeared.

c) This paragraph was included to tell the reader that the information about Atlantis's existence is based upon a legend.

d) This paragraph was included to alert the reader that Atlantis was at war with other nations in 9000 BCE.

2. What can the reader infer from the information in the "Did Atlantis Exist?" section?

a) The reader can infer that Plato wanted to memorialize Santorini through the story of Atlantis.

b) The reader can infer that Atlantis was destroyed by an earthquake or volcano.

c) The reader can infer that there is more evidence supporting the view that Atlantis did exist.

d) The reader can infer that there are two distinct theories concerning the existence of Atlantis.

3. Which sentence from the section "The Search for Atlantis: The Northeast Atlantic" would best support Plato's claim that Atlantis sank into the sea in 9000 BCE?

a) "In 1949, Dr. Maurice Ewing, aboard the research vessel *Glomar Challenger*, found an ocean-floor formation in the Northeast Atlantic, later dubbed the Horseshoe Seamounts."

b) "Its highest peak was a volcano that had collapsed beneath the sea in the past 12,000 years."

c) "In 1974, cameras aboard a Soviet research vessel captured a series of images resembling the partial remains of human-made ruins."

d) "Most (human-made remains) appeared around the peak of Mount Ampere, around 65 meters below the surface."

Check your answers. Were you correct?

1. c) is the best answer. The introductory paragraph begins to answer the first question posed in this excerpt: "What was Atlantis?" It is important to know the basis for Atlantis's existence is rooted in legends, which are traditional stories sometimes regarded as historical, yet unauthenticated.

2. d) is the best answer. After rereading this section of text, it is clear the author has presented two theories. He wants me to know that consensus has not been reached on Atlantis's existence.

3. b) is the best answer. The time reference (in the past 12,000 years) best supports Plato's claim that Atlantis sank in 9000 BCE. This underwater formation would appear to have sunk within the timeframe suggested by Plato.

Expert Reader: I'm satisfied with my responses. In all cases, I returned to the text to check against evidence. Sometimes, the evidence was right there—explicitly stated or apparent. Other times, I had to dig a little deeper and use clues and inferences. In either case, my answers square with the evidence. Now I feel I'm ready to try a constructed response question.

Question: Do you think Atlantis existed or not? Based on the evidence provided, which position do you feel is best supported? Could

Effective reading responses are constructed by returning to the text to check understanding against evidence, both explicitly stated and inferred.

you defend your claim in a discussion or through a written response using evidence from the text?

In the seventeenth century, Athanasius Kircher said he had discovered a true map of Atlantis, dating from 400 BCE, in the Vatican Library. In 1949, researchers found a ocean-floor formation in the Northeast Atlantic that matched the description of Atlantis from legend. This being said, I still feel that there is no hard, solid evidence to support the existence of Atlantis. At the time the map was supposedly made, Atlantis did not exist, as it was supposed to have sunk in 9000 BCE.

The map could have been made based on Plato's stories alone and not because it was an actual place. Similarly, the formations found underwater in 1949 included a volcano that collapsed into the sea, which is similar to the story told by Plato. However, that volcano could really be any volcano. It does not necessarily have to be the volcano from Atlantis that Plato described. The evidence presented so far has not convinced me that Atlantis was a real place.

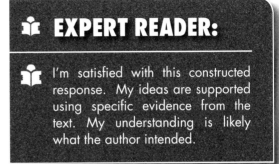

EXPERT READER:

I'm satisfied with this constructed response. My ideas are supported using specific evidence from the text. My understanding is likely what the author intended.

Conclusion

How well do you feel you've grasped the expert reader's use of the tips and tricks to analyze text and cite evidence in informational text? If you feel you're ready, move on to the guided practice in the next chapter. If you're uncertain, take another pass through the expert reader's model.

CHAPTER 5

ANALYZING TEXT AND CITING EVIDENCE IN INFORMATIONAL TEXT: GUIDED PRACTICE

Now, it's time for you to apply the tips and trick during your close reading of a passage. The practice prompt icons will guide you. Check to see if your responses to the prompts match possible responses provided.

How was Atlantis Destroyed?

 GUIDED PRACTICE PROMPT:

What jump-start clues do you notice? (Possible response: Bolded headings/subheadings help me focus on important ideas. The question/answer format continues. I'll look for evidence to help answer the questions.)

Comets and Asteroids

Atlantologists point to two major cometary impacts that could have destroyed Atlantis. The first was in about 2200 BC and the second in 1198 BC. This seems to agree with historical records. Altantologists believe that Atlantis may have survived the 2200 BC disaster, but that its final end came with the bigger catastrophe of 1198 BC, which brought an end to the Bronze Age. Geologists estimate that asteroids struck the eastern North Atlantic in that year, with global effects.

Legacy of Atlantis:
North Africa and Europe

Egypt

In about 3100 BC, Egypt began its swift rise from a simple farming society to a sophisticated civilization that built temples, developed a written language and excelled in science, engineering, and the arts. Atlantologists have argued that this transformation came about due to the arrival of Atlantean refugees in the Nile Valley, following the destruction of their homeland.

Atlantologists offer different kinds of evidence to support this argument. For example, they point to the Egyptian myth of Thaut. Thaut, it is said, arrived in Egypt at the dawn of their civilization bearing tables of knowledge. He was fleeing a flood that overwhelmed his homeland.

Basques

The Basques of the Pyrenees speak of their prehistoric forefathers as inhabitants of Atlaintika. They were said to have sailed from the "Green Isle," a powerful seafaring nation that sank into the Atlantic. The Basque

> ### 🖥 GUIDED PRACTICE PROMPT:
>
> What are you thinking? (Possible response: I know comets/asteroids can cause extreme damage. Geologists [scientists] believe an asteroid hit the North Atlantic. Atlantis may have been destroyed in this manner.)
>
> Why did the author use the word "legacy" in this heading? (Possible response: A legacy is something that continues to exist after something has ended. Is there more evidence for me to consider that supports Atlantis's existence?)

GUIDED PRACTICE PROMPT:

↗ Key in to the words the author is using—are they establishing credibility? (Possible response: "Atlantologists say" doesn't sound totally credible. Are Atlantologists real scientists? Can stories passed down from one generation to another be considered valid evidence of Atlantis's existence?)

↗ Are you thinking about the author's perspective? (Possible response: The evidence suggesting the people of Atlantis survived and relocated seems based mostly on myths and stories, not facts.)

language, Euskara, in unrelated to any Indo-European tongue, but shares similarities with the language of Guanches, natives of the Canary Islands, and Nahuatl, the language of the Aztecs. All this, Atlantologists say, suggests a link to the Atlantean culture. ↗

Maya

According to Mayan tradition, the Maya's first city, Mayapan, was founded by Chumael-Ah-Canule, the "First After the Flood." He escaped the Hun Yecil, the "drowning of the trees," that engulfed his island kingdom across the Atlantic Ocean. The temple frieze at the Mayan city of Tikal begins with the image of a man rowing his boat away from an island city tumbling into the sea during a volcanic eruption. ↗

Fact Hunter

The Horseshoe Seamounts

Could this be Atlantis? The island's dimensions seem similar to those given by Plato. Mount Ampere stands to the south, the same position assumed by Mount Atlas in Plato's description.

Why hasn't Atlantis been found yet? If a ruined city does exist on Mount Ampere, it will be under many layers of silt, mud, and possibly lava rock. No device currently available is capable of penetrating such thickly layered obstacles.

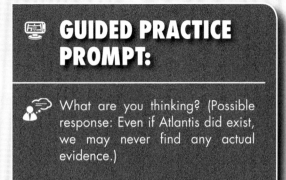

GUIDED PRACTICE PROMPT:

What are you thinking? (Possible response: Even if Atlantis did exist, we may never find any actual evidence.)

If we do penetrate the silt, what will we find? Probably very little. Even if Atlantis is down there, the cataclysm that destroyed it, if powerful enough to sink an entire island, is unlikely to have left much in the way of cultural evidence.

Quick Check Self-Evaluation for Analyzing Texts

At this point, you should be able to summarize the remaining information about Atlantis. Go ahead and try it. Talk through your answer or jot it down on a separate piece of paper. Be sure to look closely at the expert reader's take below.

Once you're satisfied and have checked your responses, challenge your thinking and answer the multiple-choice and constructed response questions that follow.

Expert Reader's Summary: One theory about Atlantis is that it was destroyed when a comet or asteroid hit it. Myths and stories from several different, sophisticated cultures tell of how people arrived from an island that either flooded or sank into the ocean. Atlantologists believe these travelers were from Atlantis, however this cannot be proved. Even if Atlantis did exist, we will probably never be able to find any conclusive evidence because of the destruction that would have occurred if it was hit by an asteroid or comet.

Quick Check Self-Evaluation for Citing Evidence: Mini Assessment

1. Which of the following statements is best supported by the information in the first paragraph of this section?

   a) Historical records provide evidence that Atlantis was destroyed by comets.

   b) Historical records document two major comet impacts in approximately 2200 BCE and 1198 BCE.

   c) Historical records prove Atlantis survived a comet in 2200 BCE.

   d) Atlantologists have discovered evidence to prove Atlantis was destroyed by a comet.

2. What can a reader infer about Atlantologists after reading paragraphs two through five?

   a) Atlantologists created the Egyptian myth of Thaut.

   b) Atlantologists have been able to document the arrival of Atlantean refugees to Basque.

   c) Atlantlologists believe Atlantean refugees helped develop many civilizations.

   d) Atlantologists have linked the Basque and Egyptian languages to Atlantis.

3. Closely reread the information in the "Fact Hunter" box. What does the author want to relay to the reader in this text?

   a) The Horseshoe Seamounts' dimensions are similar to those of Atlantis given by Plato.

   b) Mount Ampere is located in the same position as Mount Atlas.

   c) A very powerful event would be needed to sink an island.

   d) We may never be able to prove or disprove the existence of Atlantis.

When constructing written responses to reading, it is important that the views discussed are supported with multiple pieces of text-based examples or evidence.

Check your answers. Were you correct?

1. b) is a general statement that can be supported by the first paragraph. Answers a, c, and d are specific statements that claim proof of Atlantis's existence, which cannot be supported by the evidence in the text.

2. c) is the correct inference. Think about what the Atlantologists are trying to prove and then look for clue words in paragraphs two through five that help with inferences like "have argued," "it is said," "they were said to have," "suggest a link" to help you arrive at the correct answer.

3. d) is the correct answer. When asked to determine what the author wants a reader to know, you must think about the whole passage to determine the central message. In this case, although there may be compelling evidence to suggest Atlantis did exist, nothing has been discovered to conclusively prove it did.

What do you think so far? Is your understanding and analysis of the passage taking shape? Did you return to the passage and find evidence to support your responses? Did your answers square with the evidence? Are you comfortable discussing or writing a response to the following constructed response question? Again, either talk through your answer or jot it down on a separate piece of paper.

Question: What did the author most want you to know after reading this text? What is the strongest evidence provided that leads you to the author's message?

As you prepare your response, keep in mind the following:
- Have you supported your views with text-based examples?
- Is your strongest evidence presented first?
- Have you provided multiple pieces of evidence, especially if you're using inferential thinking?
- Does your interpretation align with what the author likely intended?

Once you're satisfied with your response, see how the expert reader responded. You may have a different view. That's OK as long as it holds up under scrutiny and squares with the text evidence you've chosen.

Possible Response: Although there is some compelling information to suggest that Atlantis did exist, there has been no conclusive evidence found to prove its existence. Some information and stories point to the possibility that Atlantis was destroyed by a comet or asteroid and that some of its natives escaped to nearby bodies of land. Although it is unlikely that any remains of Atlantis exist if it was hit by an asteroid or comet, should there be any remains, they will be buried under many layers of silt and mud. Presently, there are no devices in existence that can peer underwater through the layers to see what lies beneath, and no one has been able to conclusively prove that Atlantis did exist.

Conclusion

How well have you grasped the tips and tricks to analyze text and cite evidence in informational text? Based on your performance and self evaluation, decide if you've mastered the skills or if you would like to take another pass through this guided practice.

A New Expert Reader!

Now that you've mastered how to use the tips and tricks for analyzing text and citing evidence, you're on your way to becoming an expert reader! Continue to practice with different types of literature and informational texts. You'll see that your attempts to grapple with classroom and assigned texts are far easier now.

GLOSSARY

ANALYZE To carefully examine, inspect, and consider a text in order to fully understand it.

CLAIM A position that one takes on a matter.

CLOSE READING The deep, analytical reading of a brief passage of text in which the reader constructs meaning based on author intention and textual evidence. The close reading of a text enables readers to gain insights that exceed a cursory reading.

DISTRACTOR Anything that steers a reader away from the text evidence and weakens or misguides analysis.

EVIDENCE Information from the text that a reader uses to prove a claim, position, conclusion, inference, or big idea.

FIX-UP STRATEGIES Common techniques used when meaning is lost.

GENRE A system used to classify types or kinds of writing.

HEADING A phrase in larger font or bold-faced print that provides information on the topic of a section of text.

INFERENCE A conclusion that a reader draws about something by using information that is available.

INFORMATIONAL TEXT A type of nonfiction text, such as articles, essays, opinion pieces, memoirs, and historical, scientific, technical, or economic accounts, that is written to give facts or inform about a topic.

LITERATURE Imaginary stories, such as mysteries, myths, science fiction, allegories, and other genres, that include elements such as characters, problems or conflicts, setting, plot with events or episodes, and problem resolution.

PERSPECTIVE The position a narrator takes in a text.

POINT OF VIEW The perspective, or position, from which the story is told.

SUBHEADING A phrase in larger font than the text that provides information about a topic of a section of text.

SUMMARY A short account of a text that gives the main points but not all the details.

TEXT FEATURES The variety of tools used to organize text and to give readers more information about the text.

TEXT STRUCTURE The way in which information is organized within a written text.

THEME The central message of a text or what the story is really about.

TONE The writer's communication of an overall feeling or attitude about a book's subject, content, or topic.

TOPIC The subject of a piece of text.

FOR MORE INFORMATION

Council of Chief State School Officers
One Massachusetts Avenue NW
Suite 700
Washington, DC 20001-1431
(202) 336-7000
Website: http://www.ccsso.org
The Common Core State Standards Initiative is a state-led effort
coordinated by the National Governors Association Center for
Best Practices (NGA Center) and the Council of Chief State
School Officers (CCSSO). The standards provide a clear and con-
sistent framework to prepare students for college and the
workforce.

National Parent Teacher Association (PTA)
12250 North Pitt Street
Alexandria, VA 22314
(703) 518-1200
Website: http://www.pta.org
The National PTA enthusiastically supports the adoption and implementation by all states of the Common Core State Standards. The
standards form a solid foundation for high-quality education.

New York State Education Department
89 Washington Avenue
Albany, NY 12234
(518) 474-3852
Website: http://www.engageny.org
EngageNY.org is developed and maintained by the New York State
Education Department. This is the official website for current mate-
rials and resources related to the implementation of the New York
State P-12 Common Core Learning Standards (CCLS).

Partnership for Assessment of Readiness for College and Careers (PARCC)
1400 16th Street NW, Suite 510
Washington, DC 20036
(202) 745-2311
Website: http://www.parcconline.org
The Partnership for Assessment of Readiness for College and Careers (PARCC) is a consortium of eighteen states plus the District of Columbia and the U.S. Virgin Islands working together to develop a common set of K–12 assessments in English and math anchored in what it takes to be prepared for college and careers.

United States Department of Education
Department of Education Building
400 Maryland Avenue SW
Washington, DC 20202
(800) 872-5327
Website: http://www.edu.gov
Nearly every state has now adopted the Common Core State Standards. The federal government has supported this state-led effort by helping to ensure that higher standards are being implemented for all students and that educators are being supported in transitioning to new standards.

Websites

Due to the changing nature of Internet links, Rosen Publishing has developed an online list of websites related to the subject of this book. This site is updated regularly. Please use this link to access the list:

http://www.rosenlinks.com/CCRGR/Evid

BIBLIOGRAPHY

Beers, Kylene, and Robert E. Probst. *Notice & Note: Strategies for Close Reading*. Portsmouth, NH: Heinemann, 2013

Fountas, Irene C., and Gay Su Pinnell. *Genre Study: Teaching with Fiction and Nonfiction Books*. Portsmouth, NH: Heinemann, 2012

Francis, Pauline. *The Odyssey: An Adventure Classic*. New York, NY: Windmill Books (Skyview Books), 2009.

Hawkins, John. *Mystery Hunters: Atlantis and Other Lost Worlds*. New York, NY: Rosen Publishing, 2012.

INDEX

About the Authors

Sandra K. Athans is a national board-certified practicing classroom teacher with fifteen years of experience teaching reading and writing at the elementary level. She is the author of several teacher-practitioner books on literacy including *Quality Comprehension* and *Fun-tastic Activities for Differentiating Comprehension Instruction*, both published by the International Reading Association. Athans has presented her research at the International Reading Association, the National Council of Teachers of English Conferences, and the New York State Reading Association Conferences. Her contributions have appeared in well-known literary works including *The Literacy Leadership Handbook* and *Strategic Writing Mini-Lessons*.

Athans earned a B.A. in English from the University of Michigan, an M.A. in elementary education from Manhattanville College, and an M.S. in literacy (birth through sixth grade) from Le Moyne College. She is also certified to teach secondary English. In addition to teaching in the classroom, she is an adjunct professor at Le Moyne College and provides instruction in graduate-level literacy classes. This spring she was named outstanding elementary social studies educator by the Central New York Council for Social Studies. Athans serves on various ELA leadership networks and collaborates with educators nationwide to address the challenges of the Common Core Standards. The Common Core Readiness Guide to Reading is among several Common Core resources she has authored for Rosen Publishing.

Robin W. Parente is a practicing reading specialist and classroom teacher with over fifteen years of experience teaching reading and writing at the elementary level. She also serves as the elementary ELA coordinator for a medium-sized district in central New York, working with classroom teachers to implement best literacy practices in the classroom. Parente earned a B.S. in elementary education and an M.S. in education/literacy from SUNY-Oswego. She is a certified reading specialist and elementary classroom teacher and has served on various ELA leadership networks to collaborate with educators to address the challenges of the Common Core Standards. The Common Core Readiness Guide to Reading is among several Common Core resources she has authored for Rosen Publishing.

Photo Credits

32.95   12/10/14

LONGWOOD PUBLIC LIBRARY
800 Middle Country Road
Middle Island, NY 11953
(631) 924-6400
longwoodlibrary.org

LIBRARY HOURS

Monday-Friday	9:30 a.m. - 9:00 p.m.
Saturday	9:30 a.m. - 5:00 p.m.
Sunday (Sept-June)	1:00 p.m. - 5:00 p.m.